Mandala Designs Coloring Book No. 3
32 New Mandala Designs

by Alberta Hutchinson

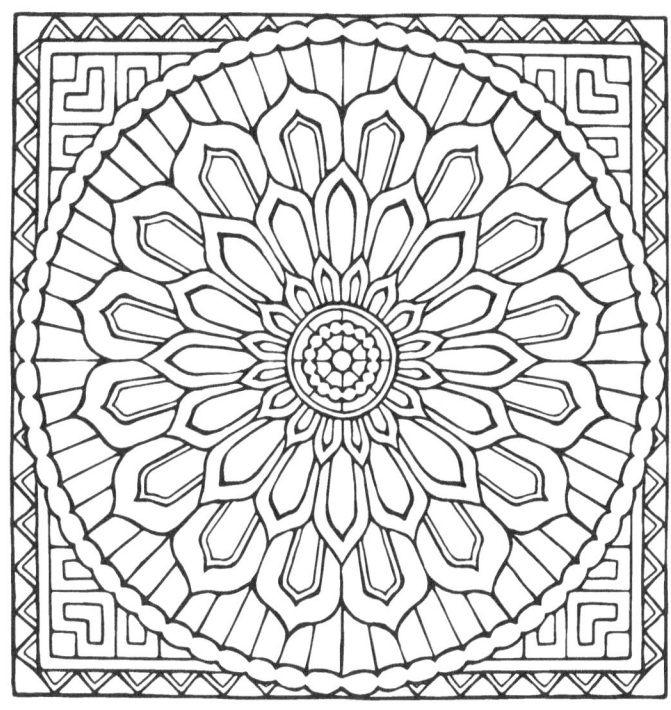

This coloring book has been revised in a new format to fit the new
Hutchinson Mandala Coloring Book Collection

A book list of the Hutchinson Collection appears in the back of this book.

Illume Writers & Artists

Copyright © 2014 by Alberta L. Hutchinson
All rights reserved

ISBN: 978-1494976606

Hutchinson Mandala Coloring Book Collection

Series:

Published by:

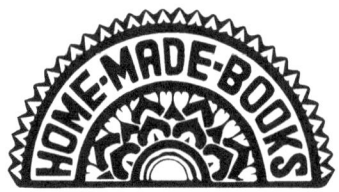

An Imprint of

Illume Writers & Artists

PO Box 86, Gilbertsville, NY 13776

Printed in the United States of America

This book belongs to the Home Made Books Sacred Design Series. You may use the designs and illustrations for personal, classroom, and nonprofit applications, free and without special permission. (For permission for additional use, please write to Illume Writers and Artists, P.O. Box 86, Gilbertsville, New York 13776. E-mail: illumewritersartists@live.com)
However, republication or reproduction of any illustration by any commercial graphic service, whether it be in a book or in any other design resource, is strictly prohibited.

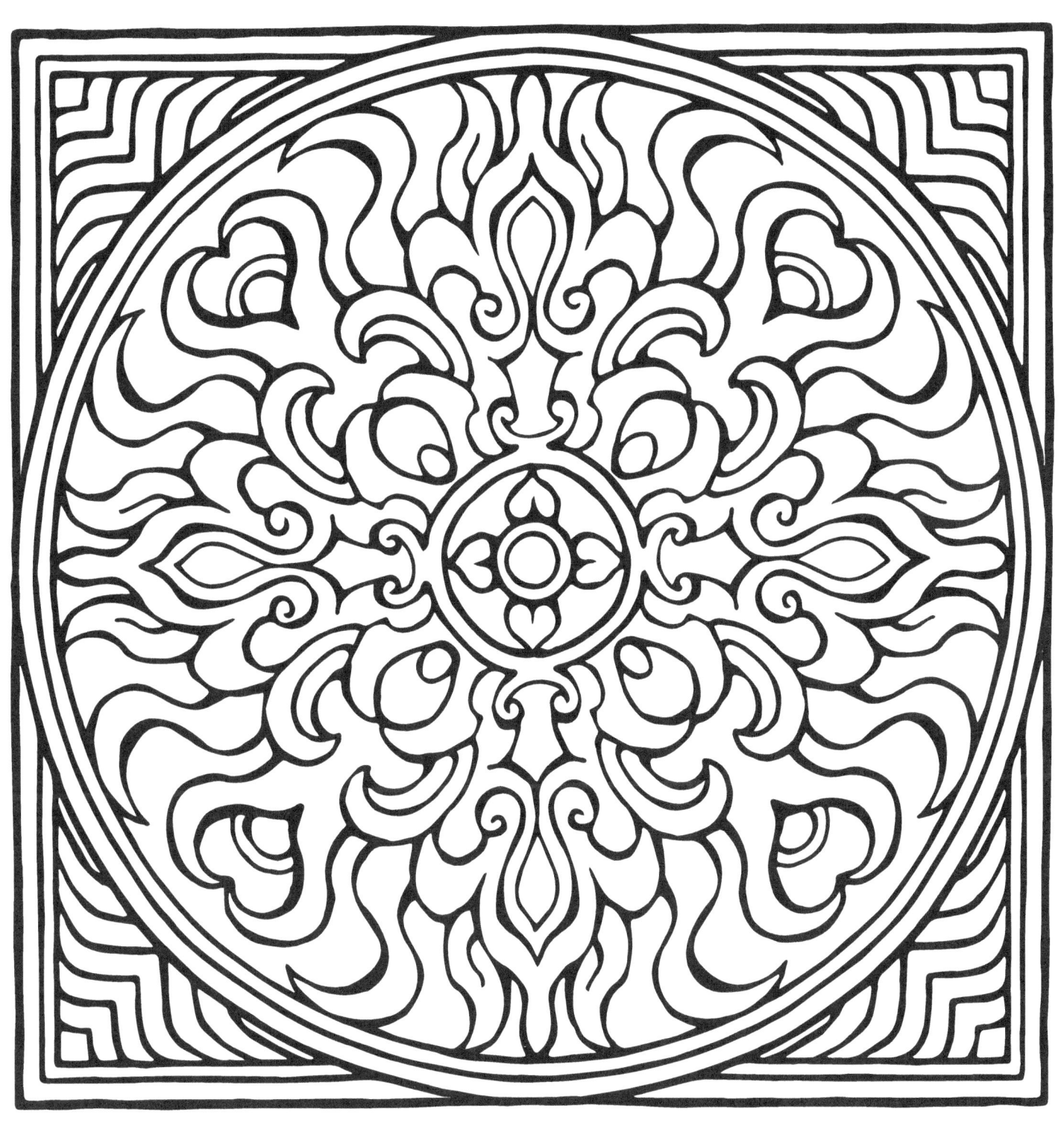

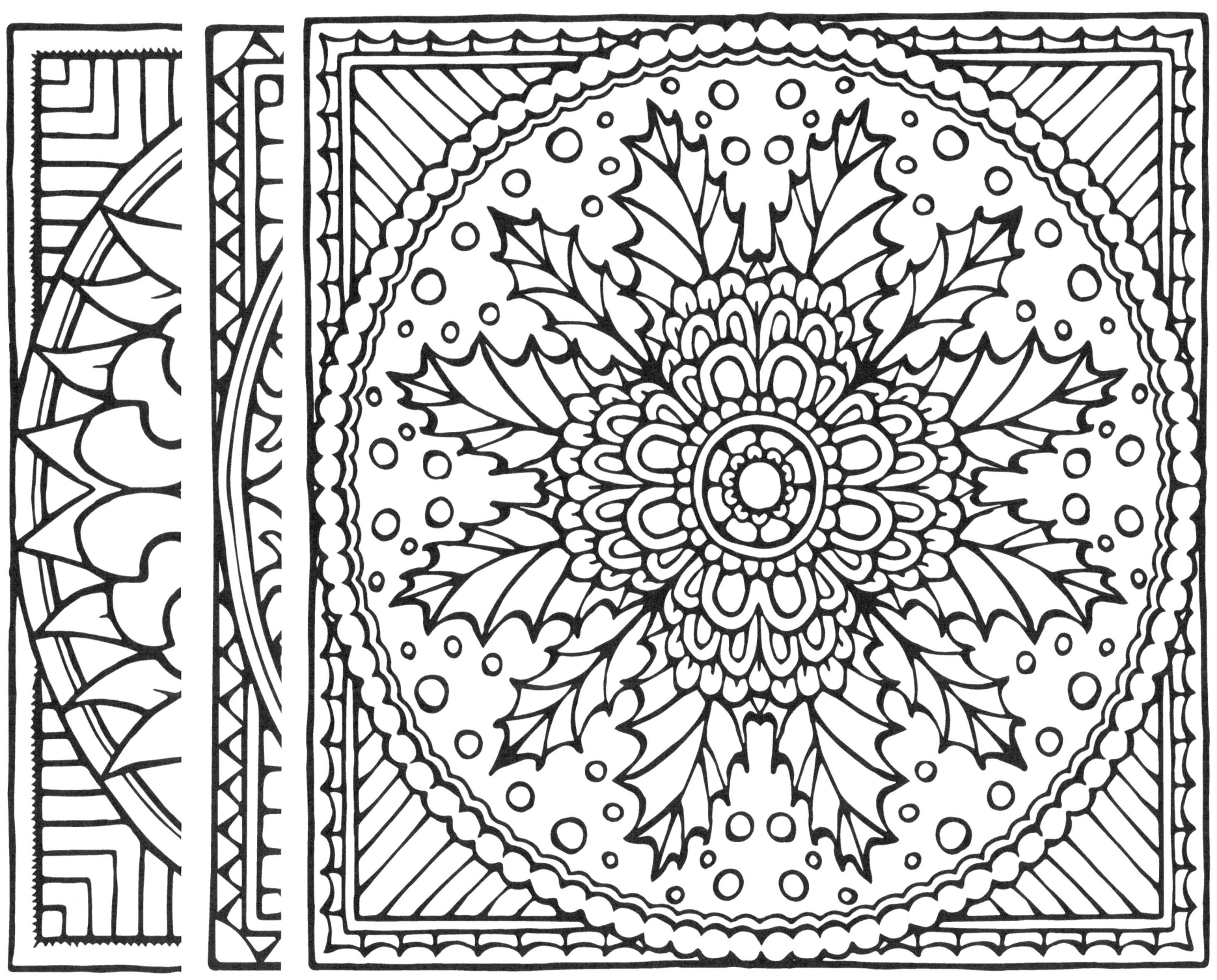

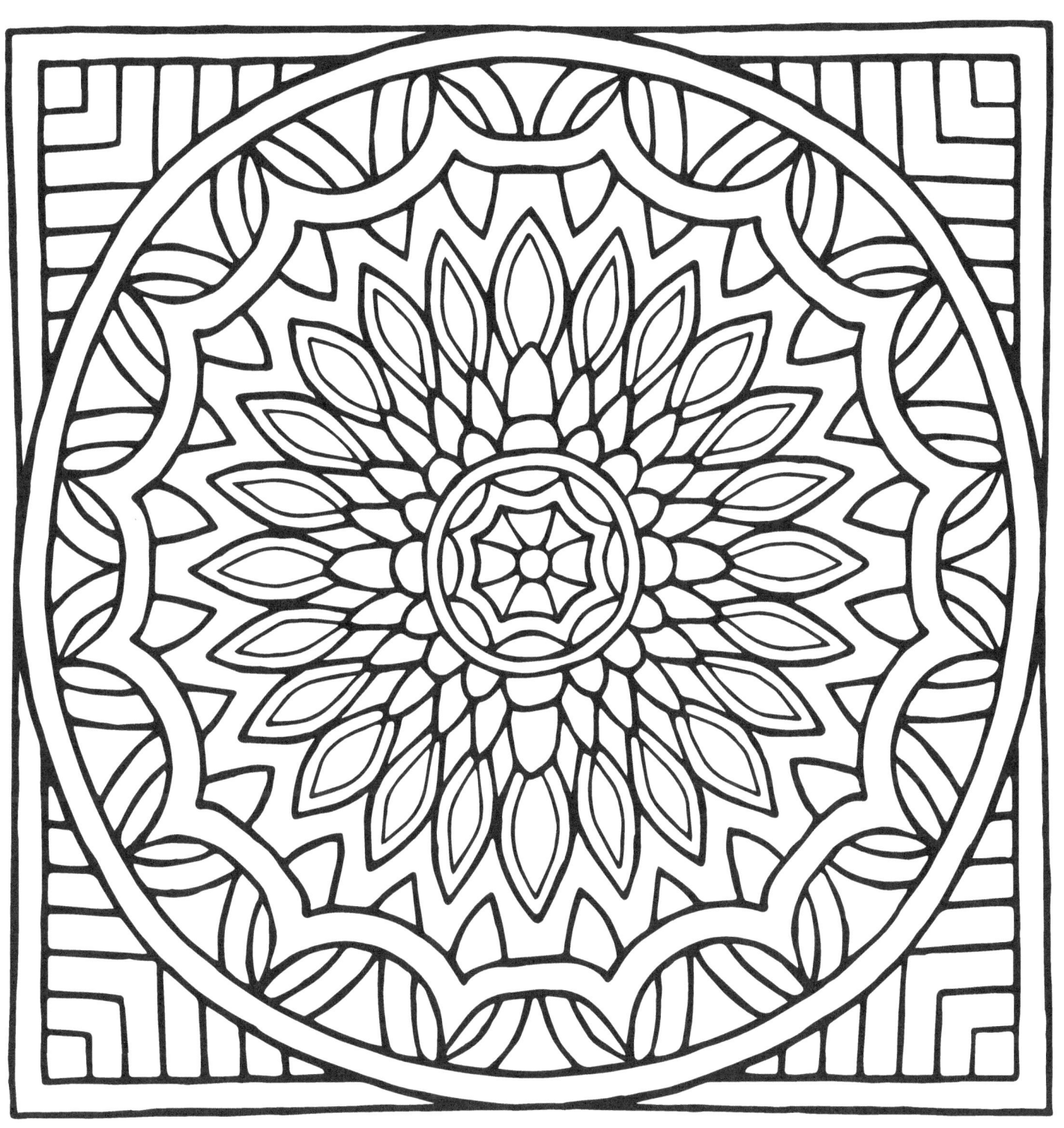

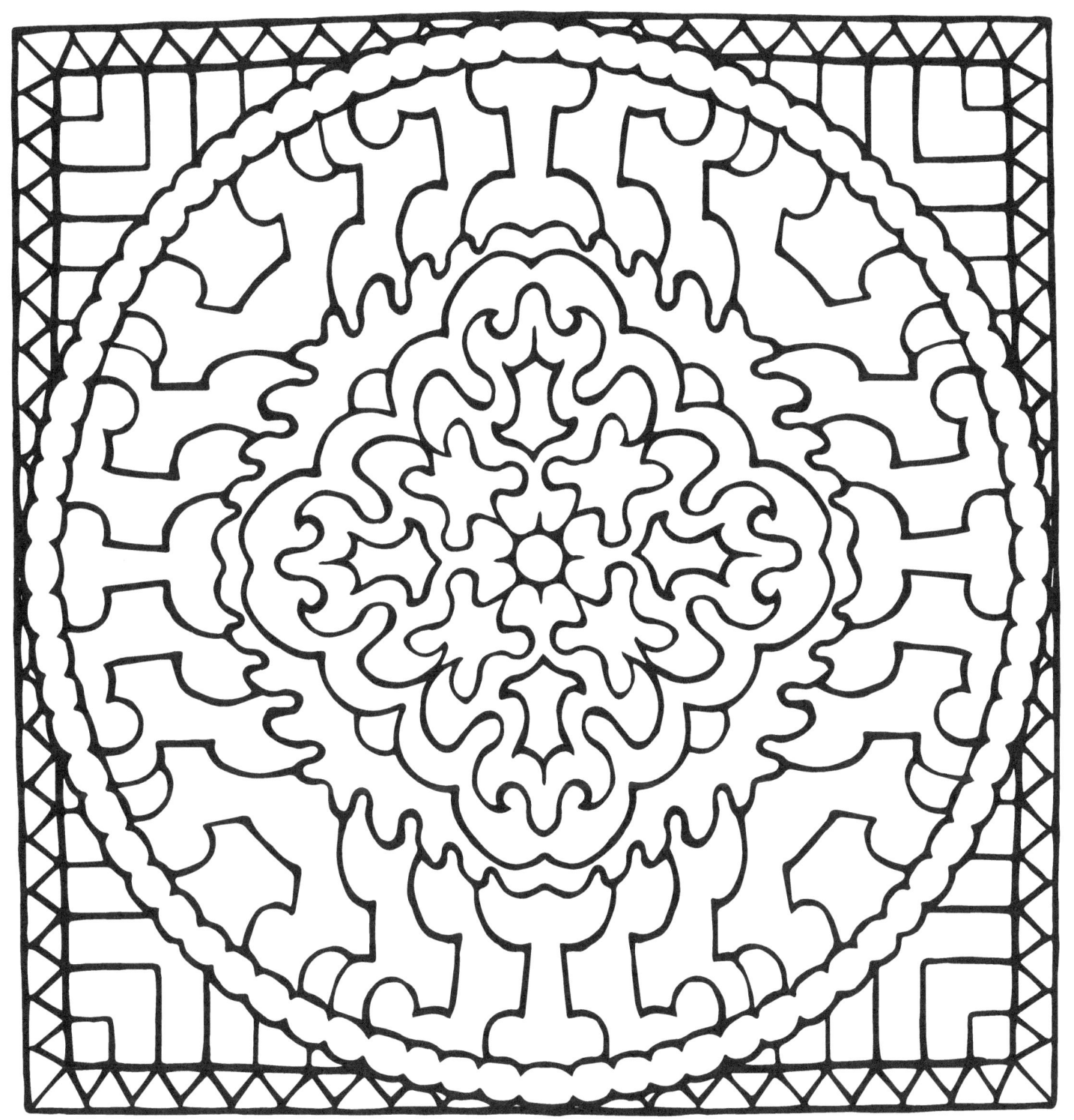

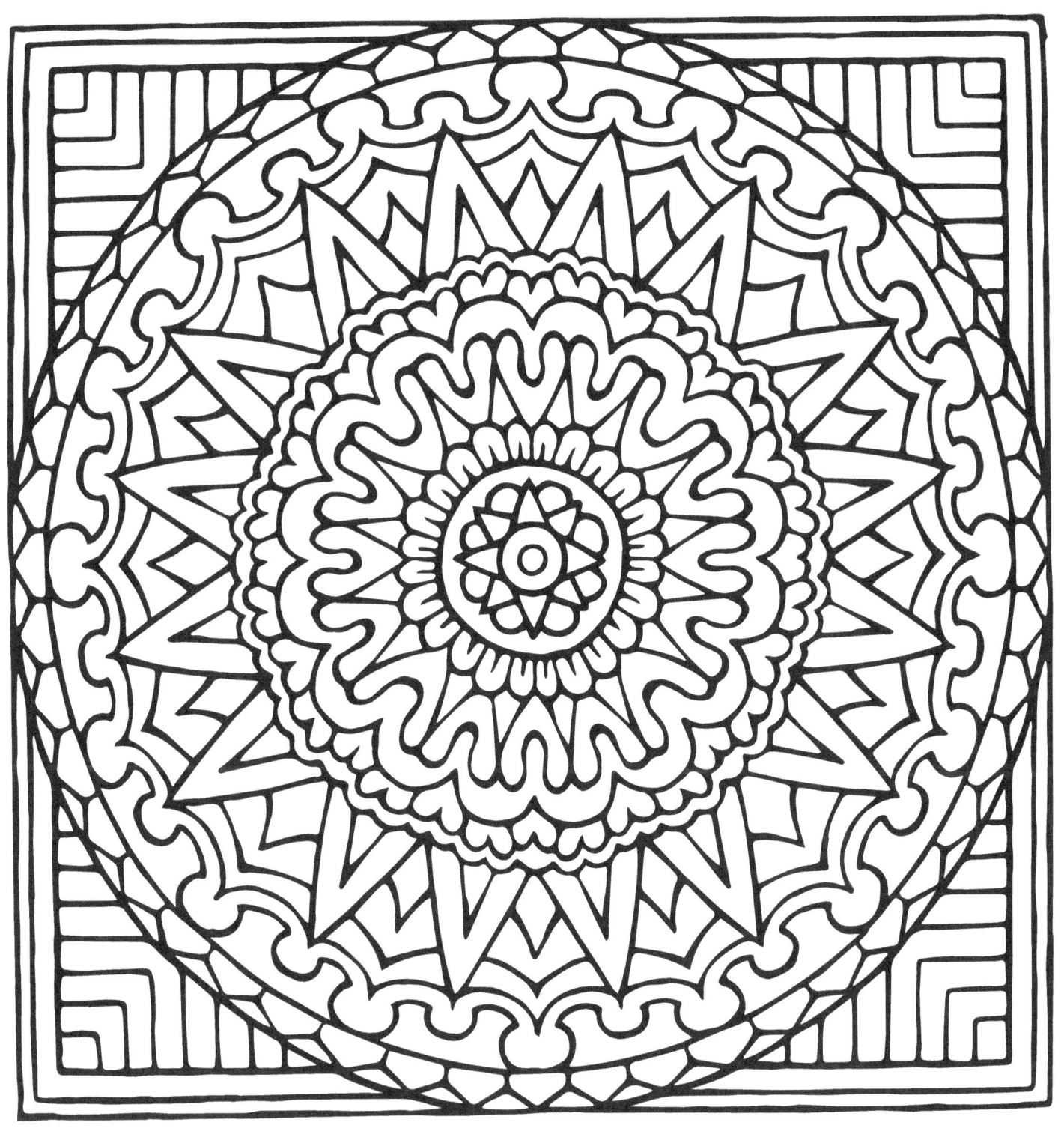

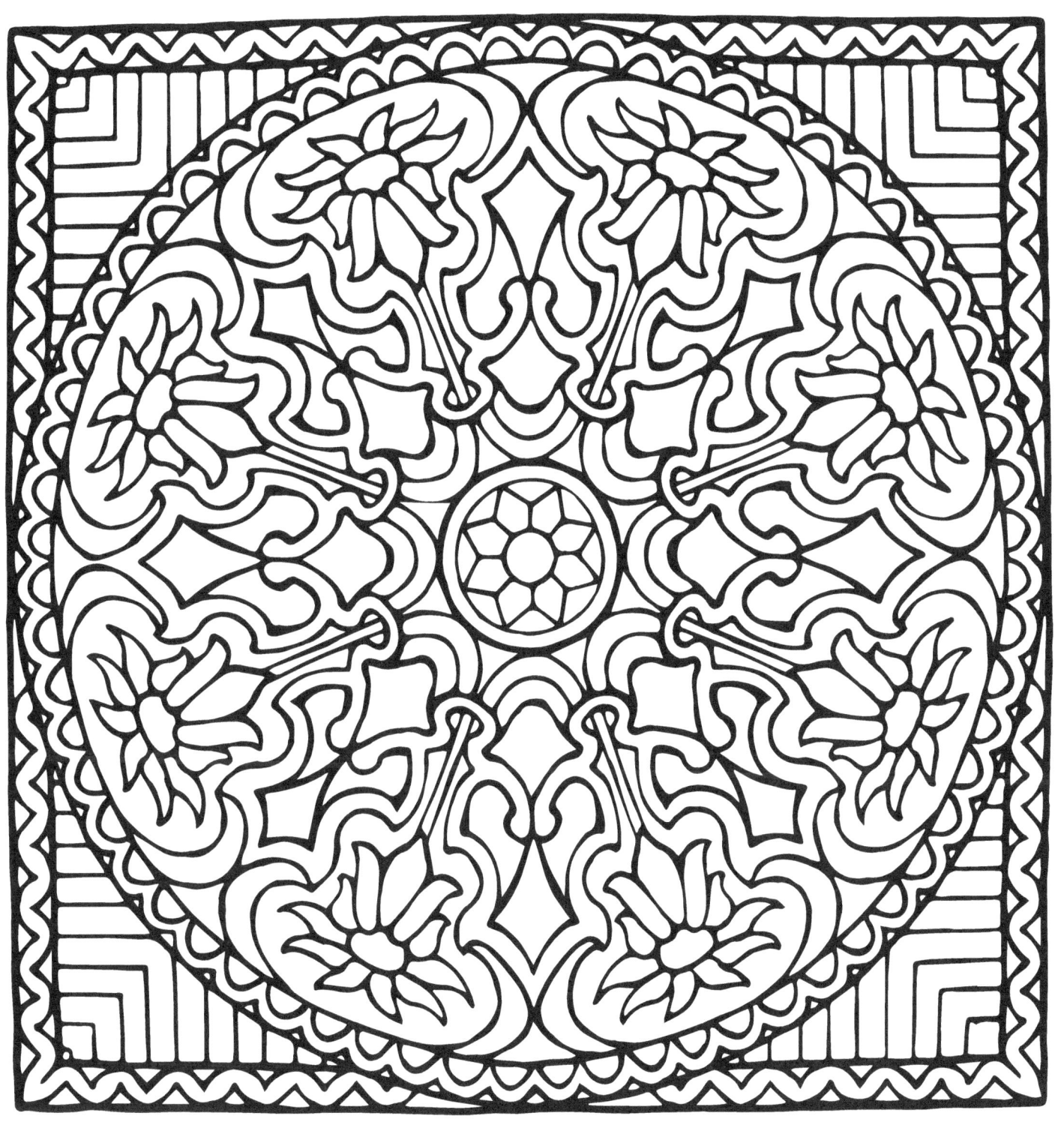

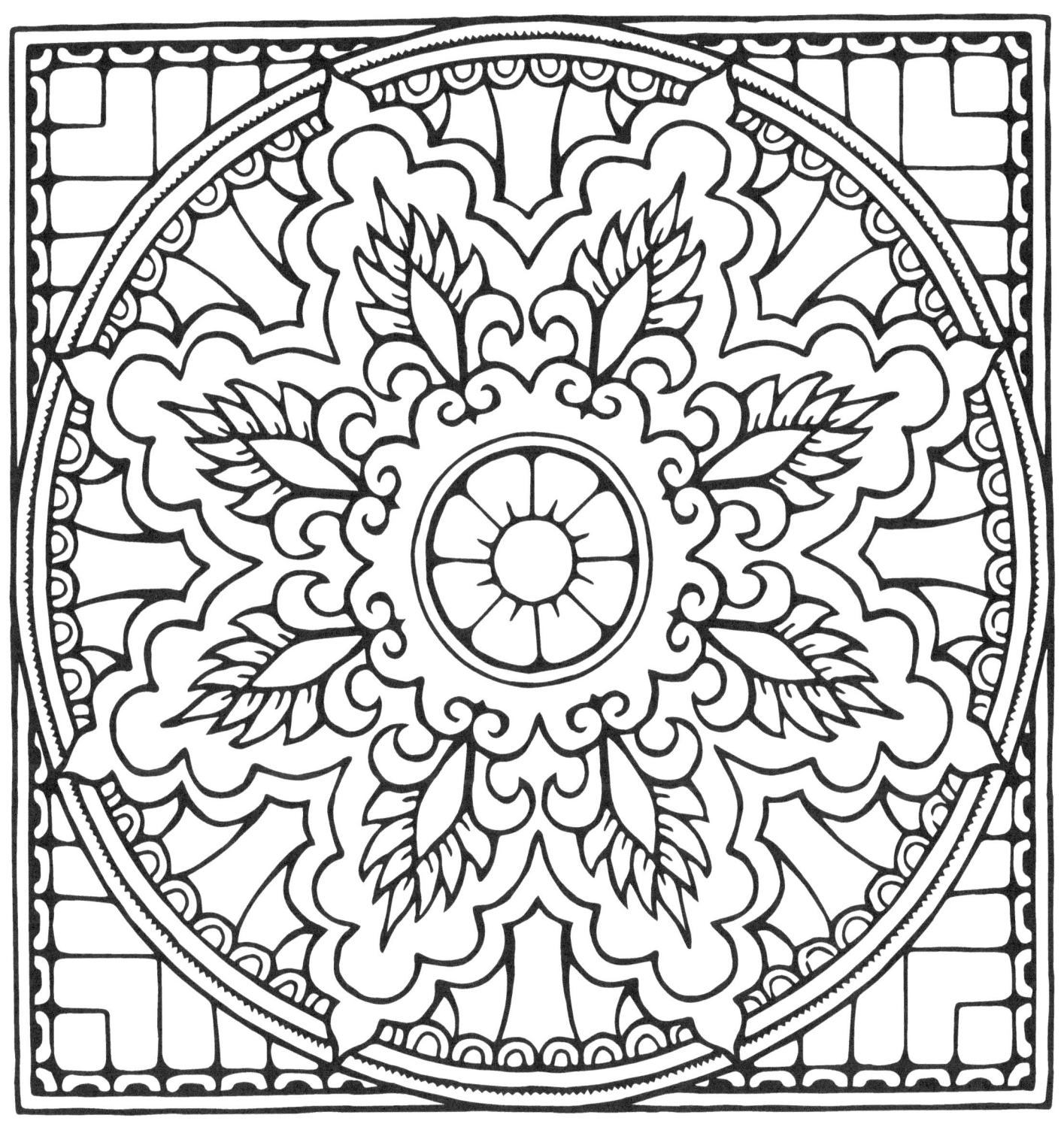

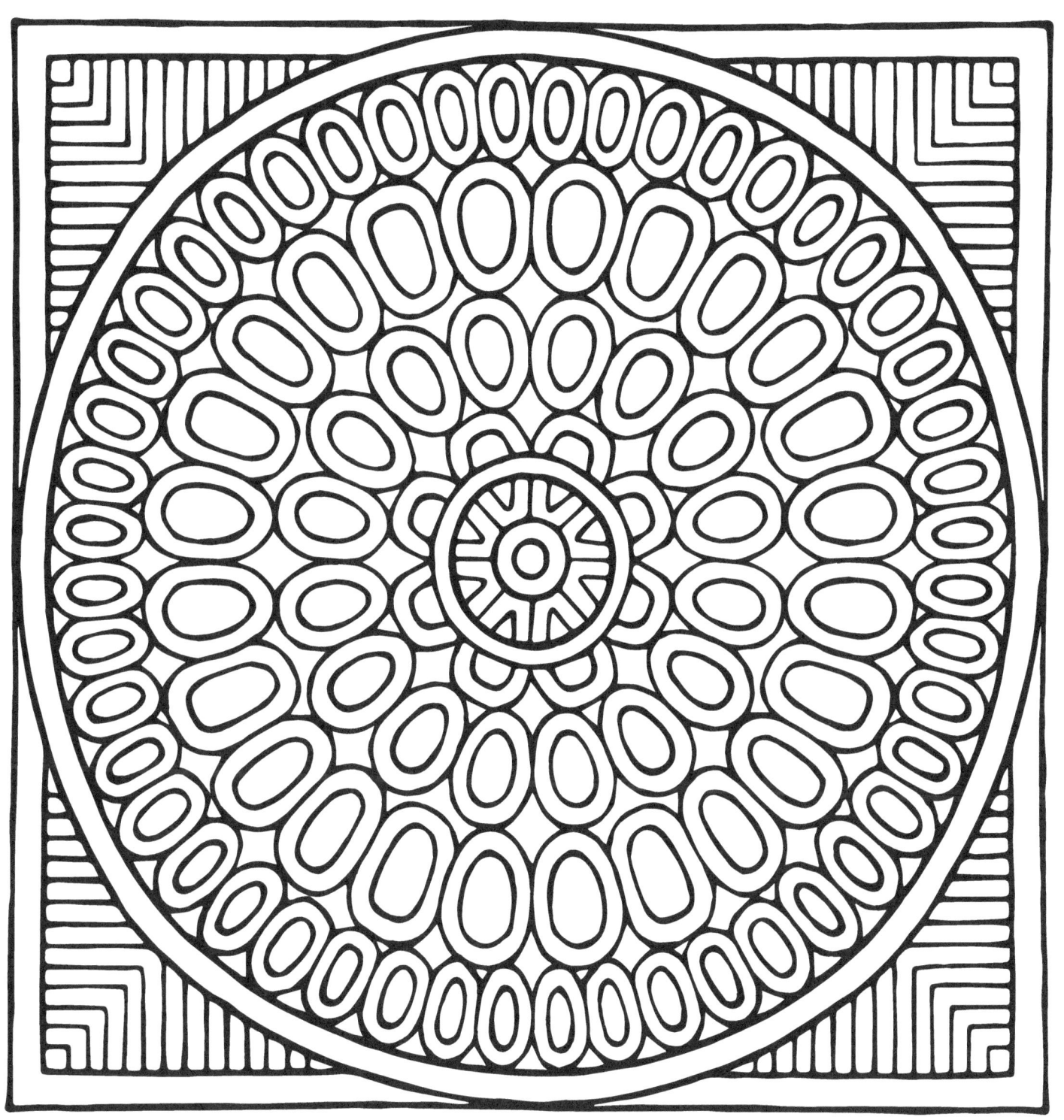

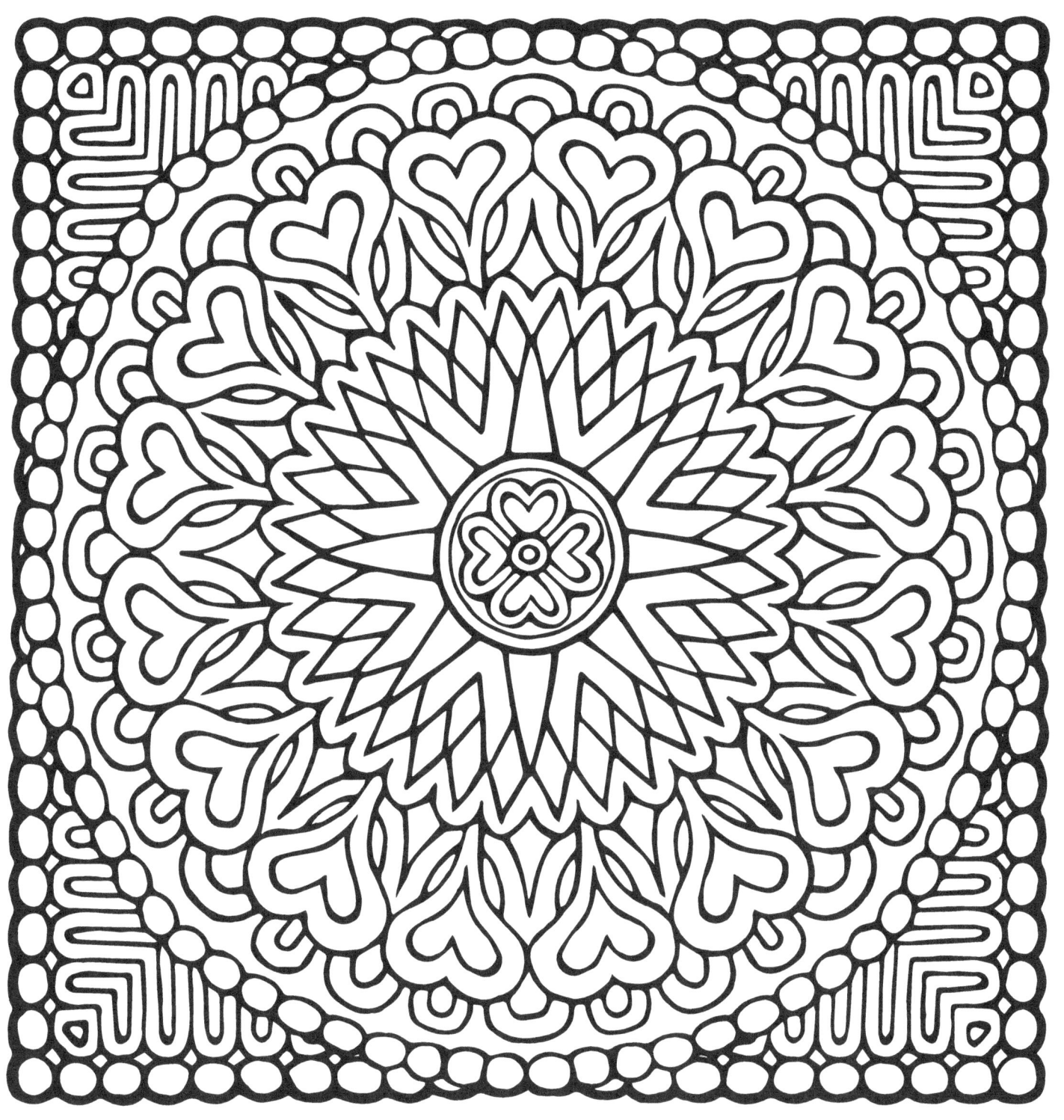

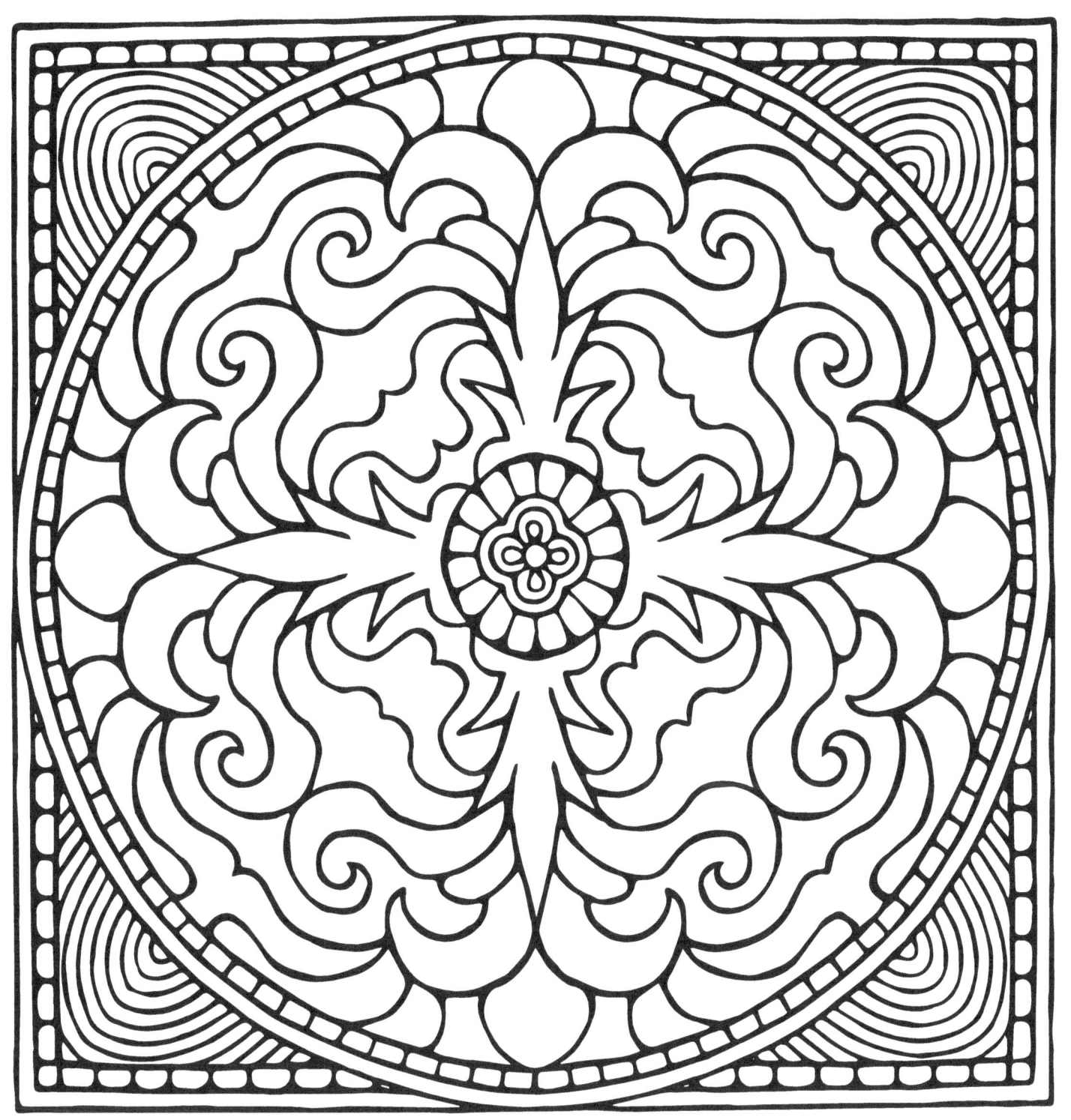

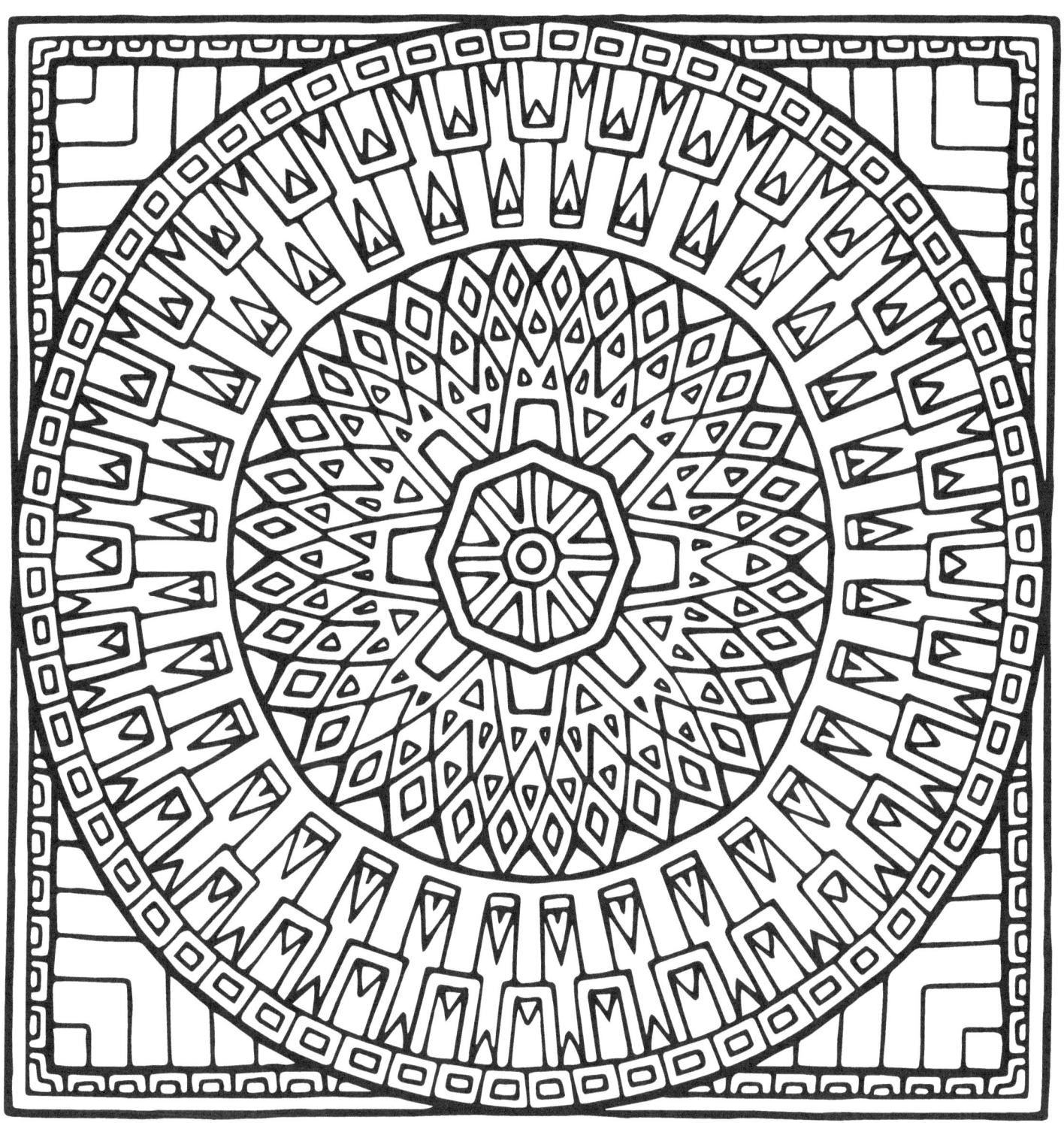

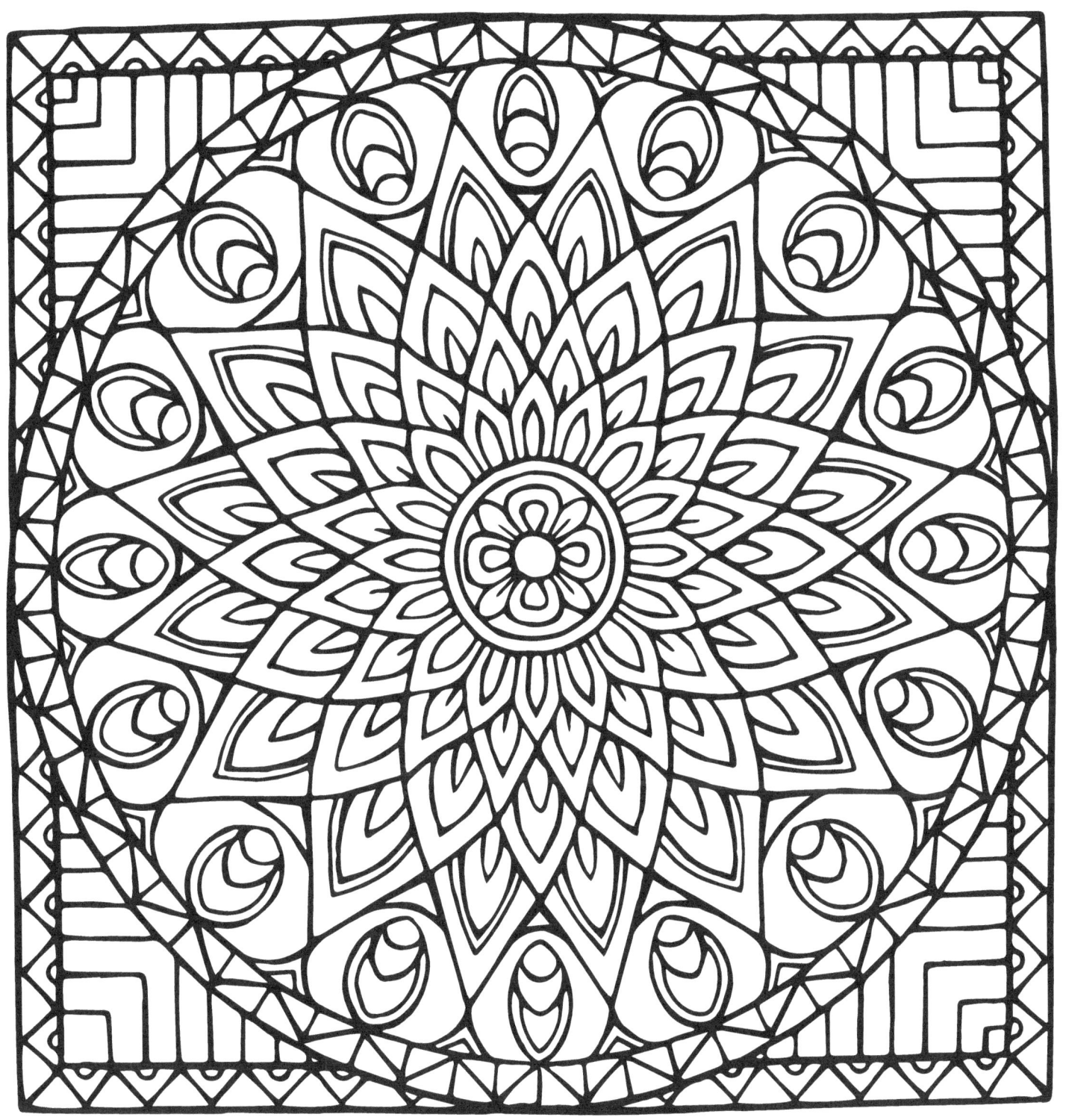

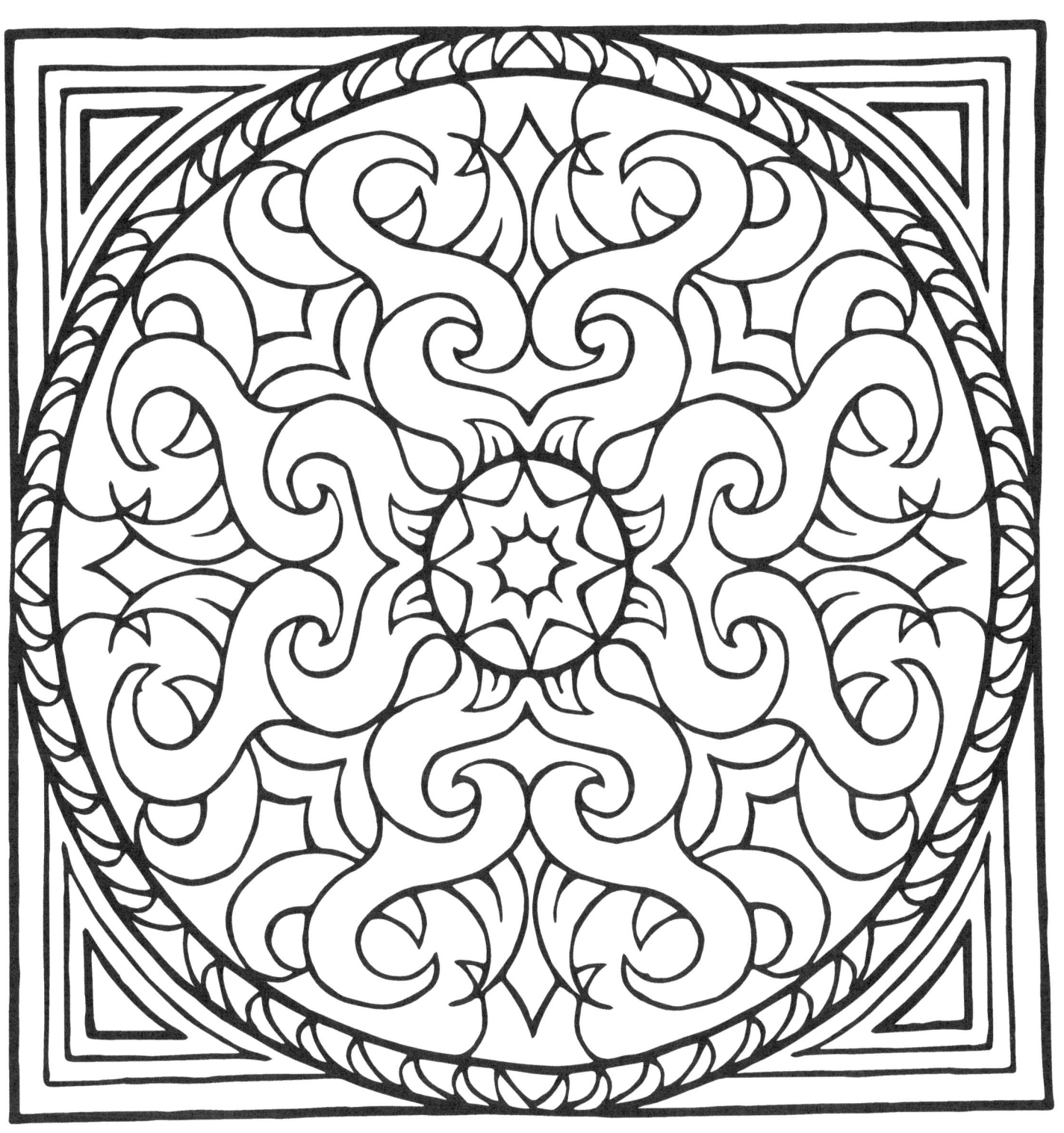

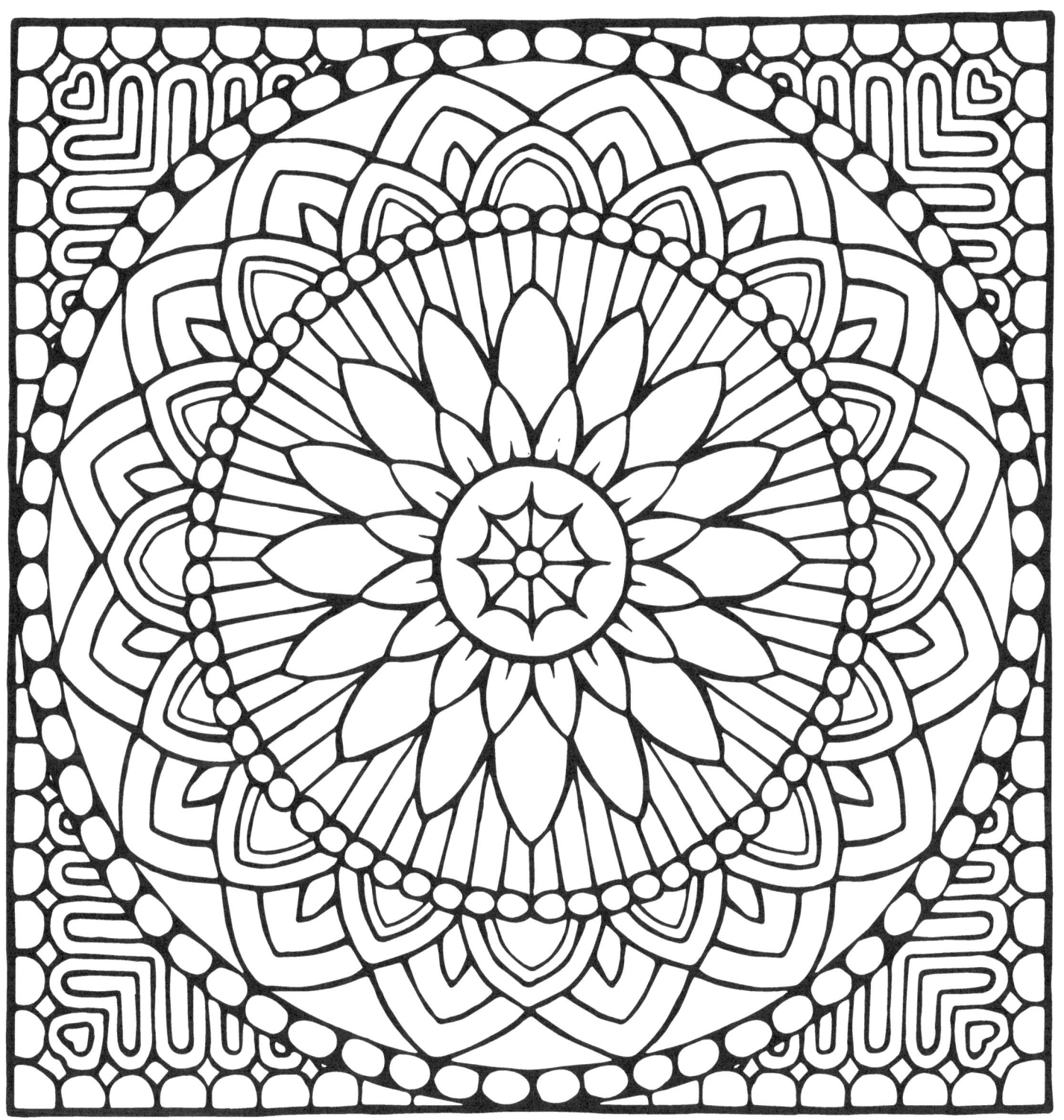

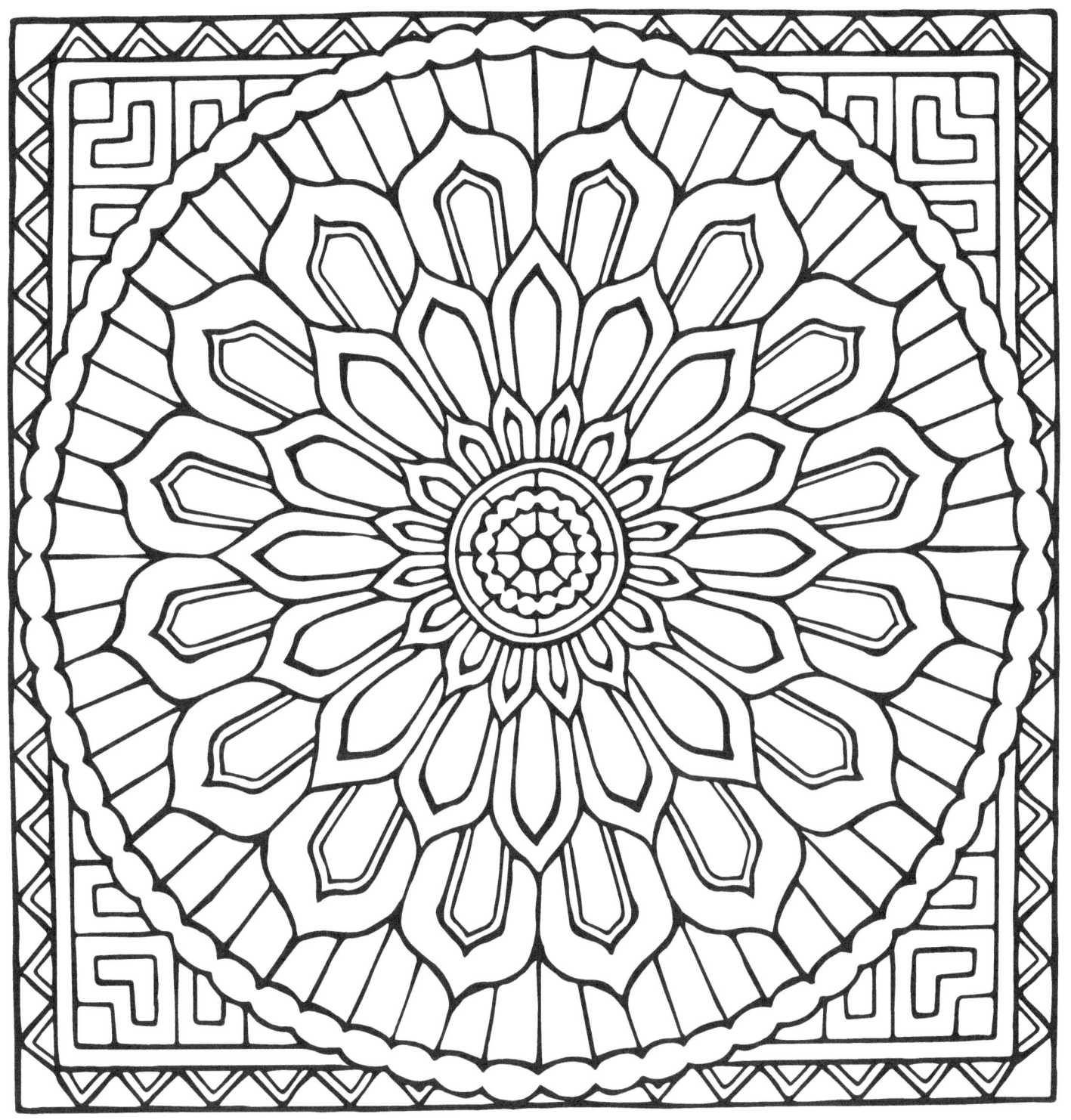

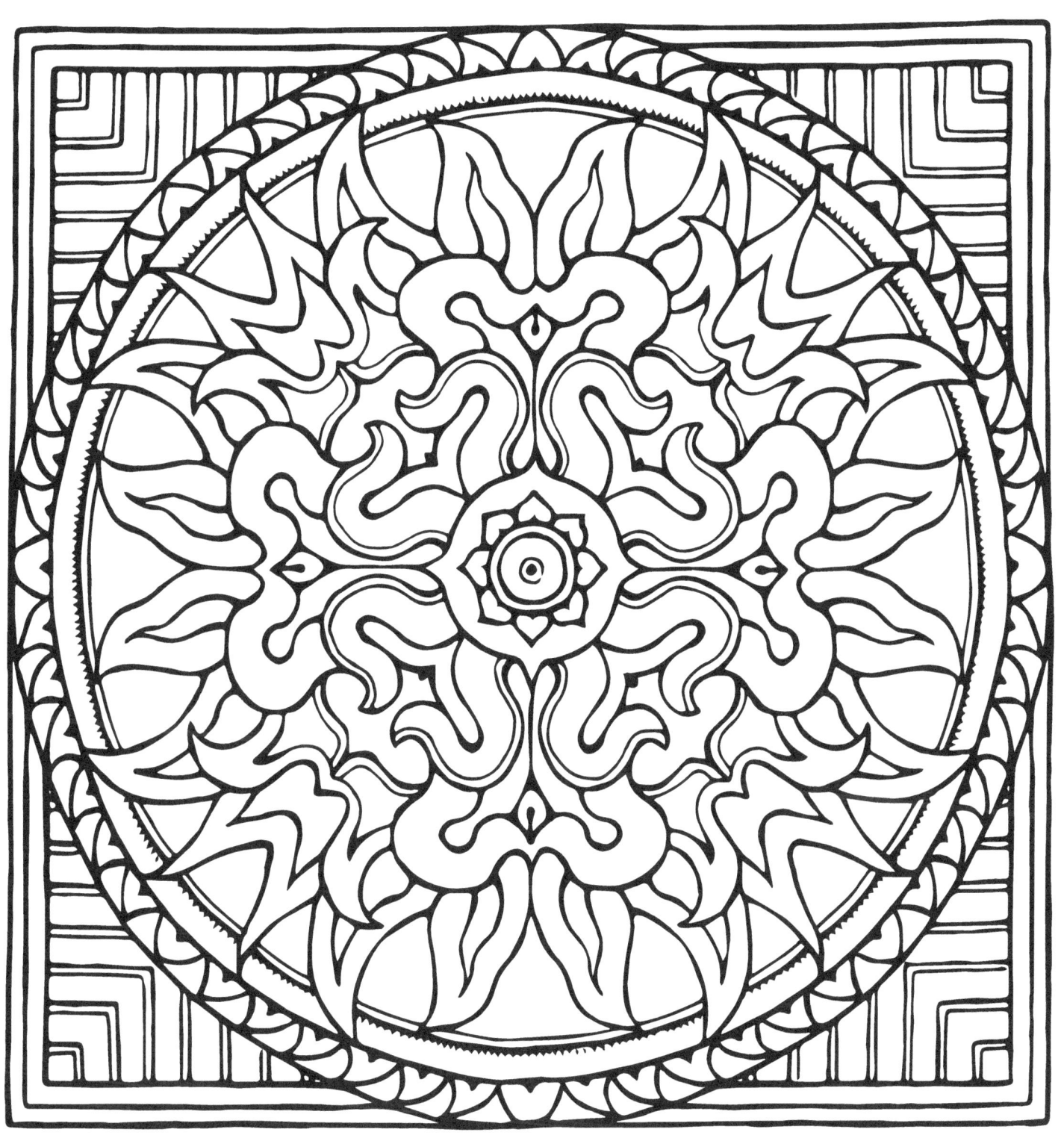

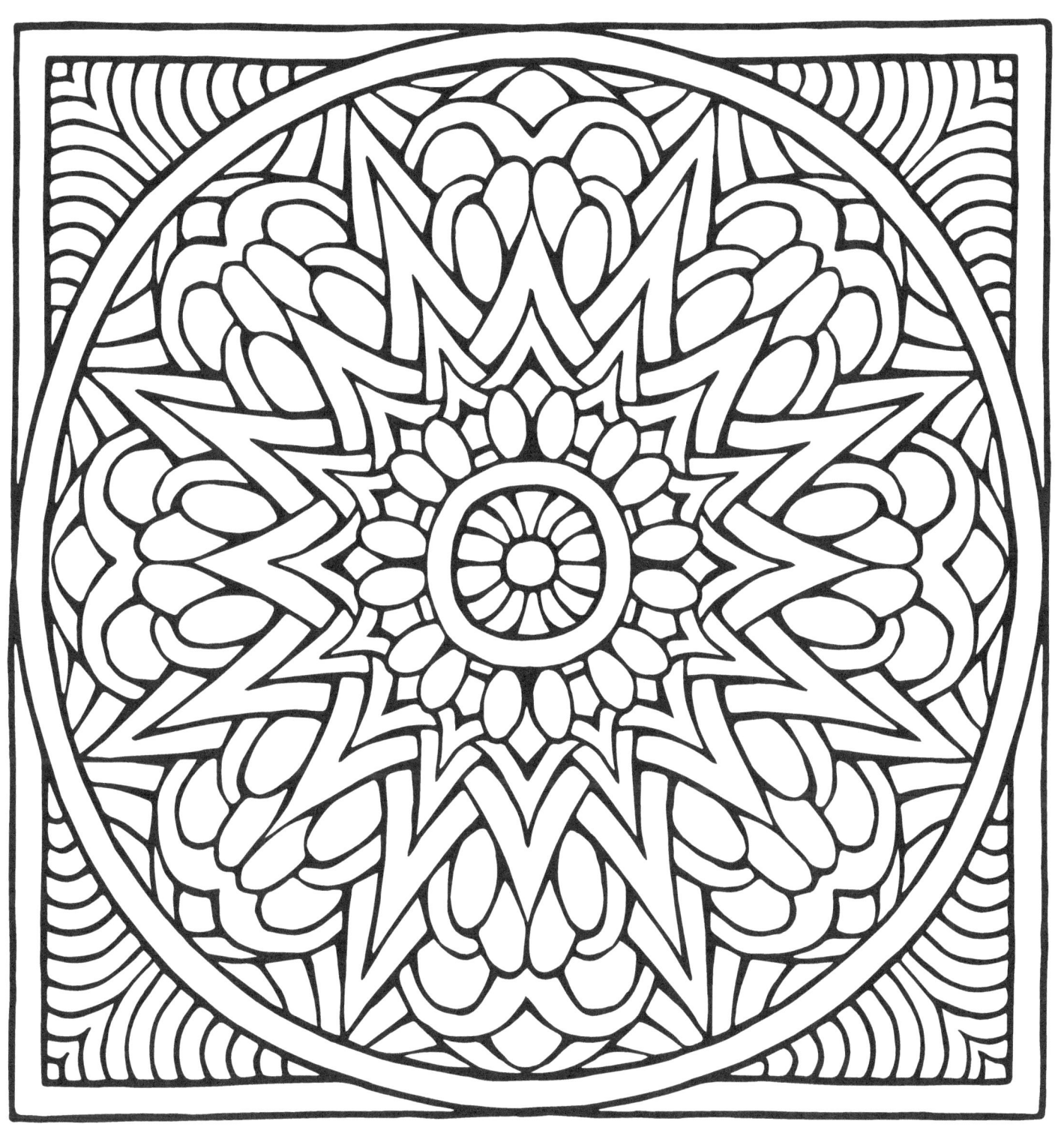

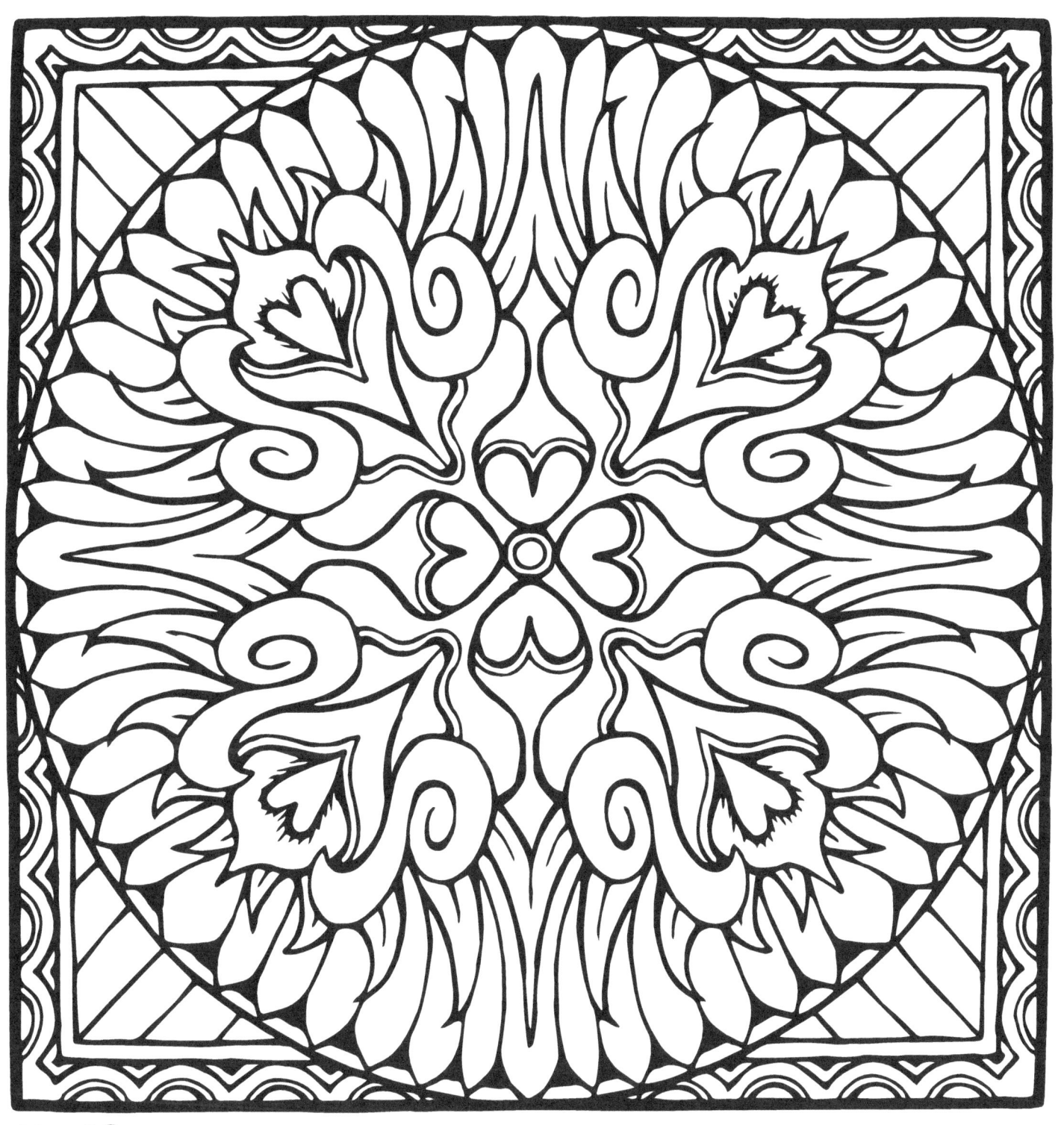

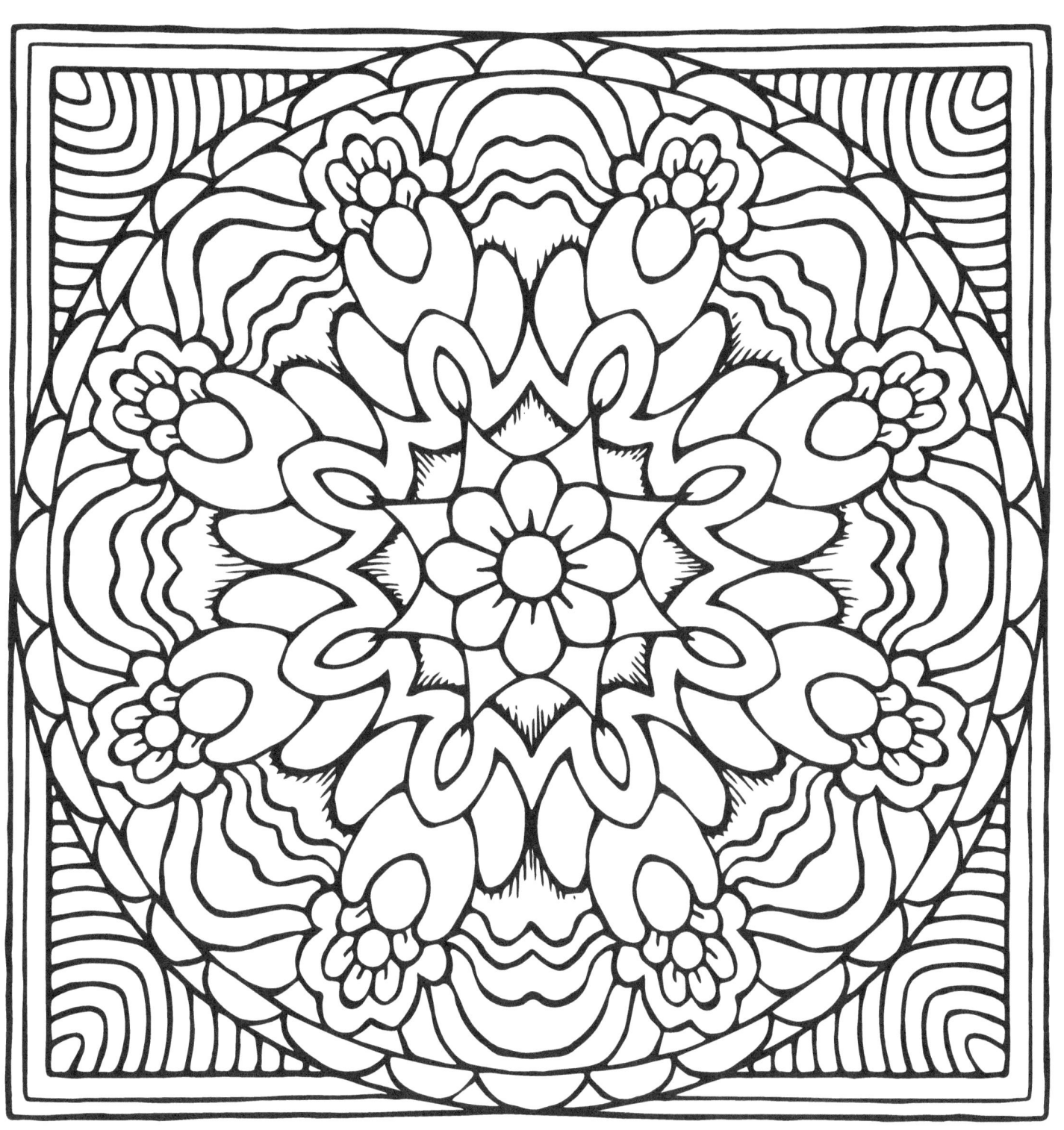

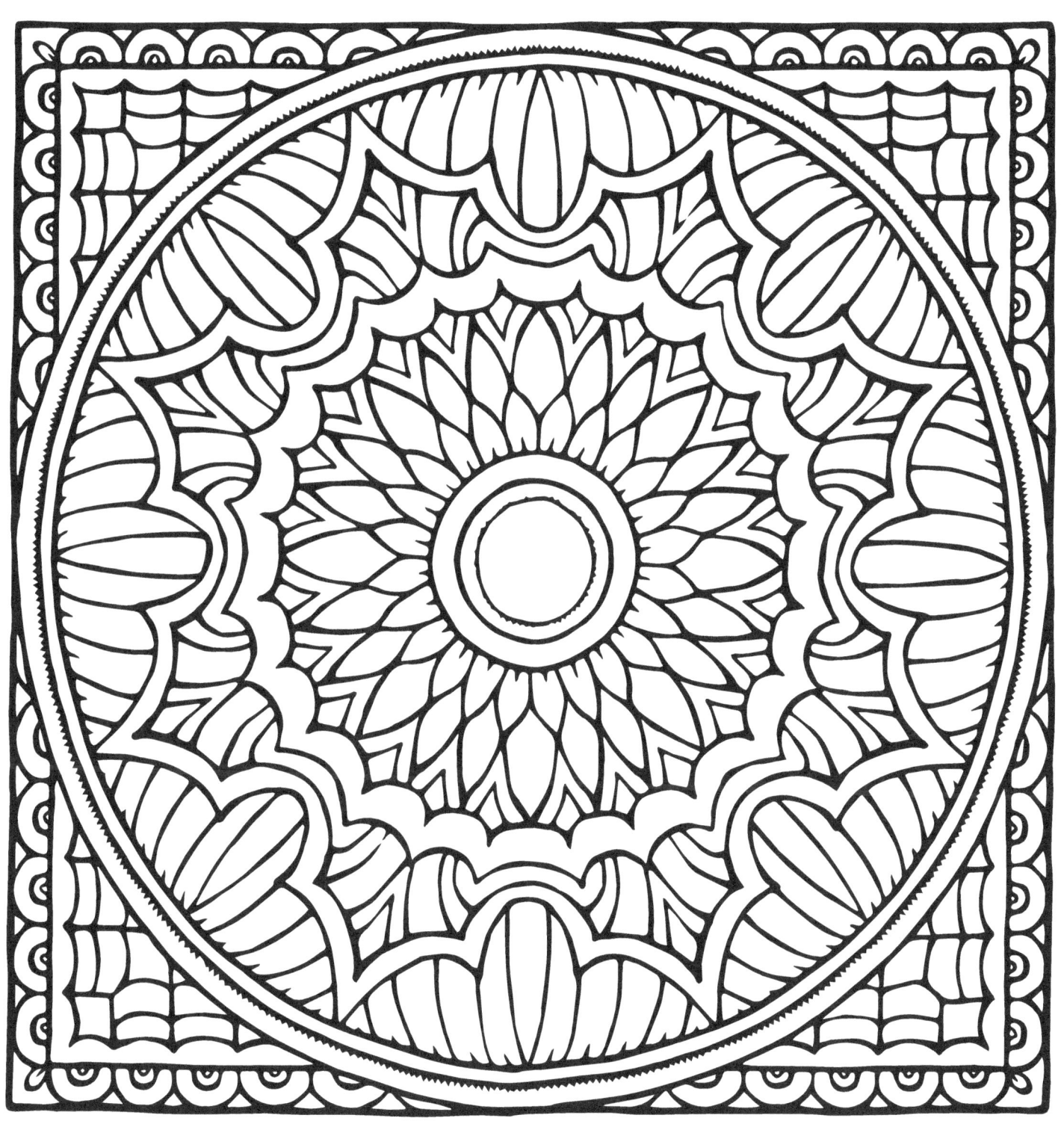

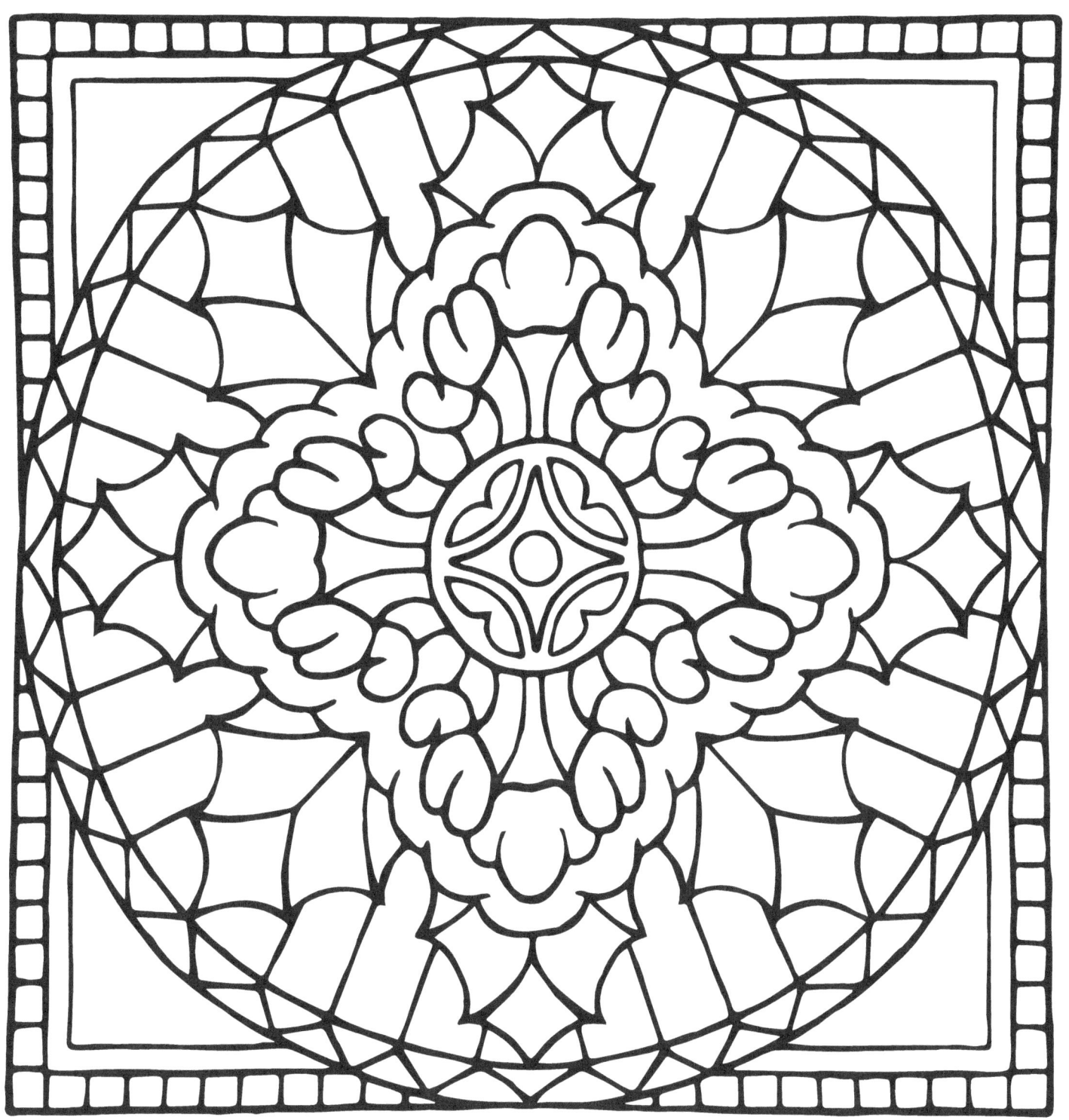

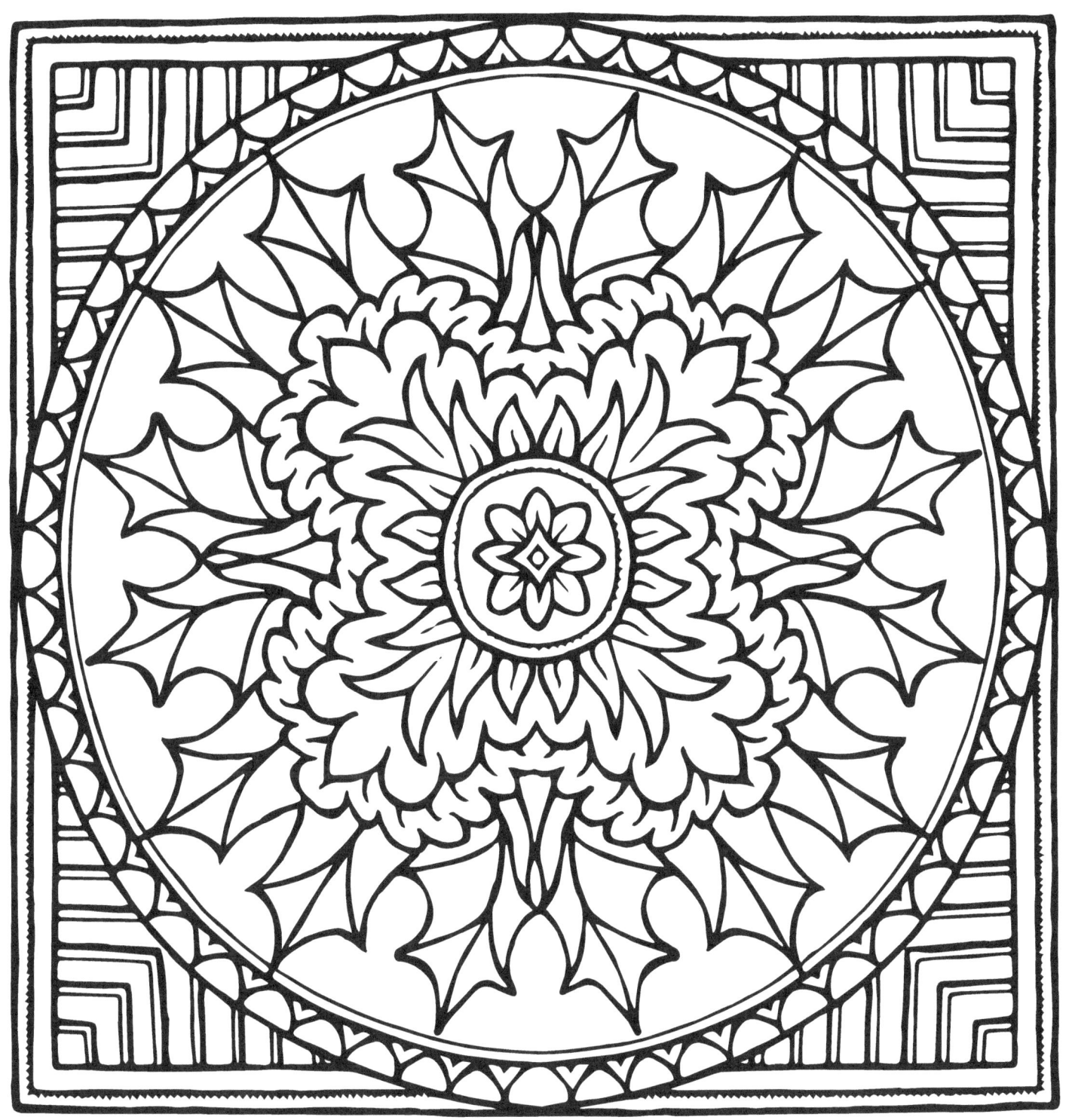

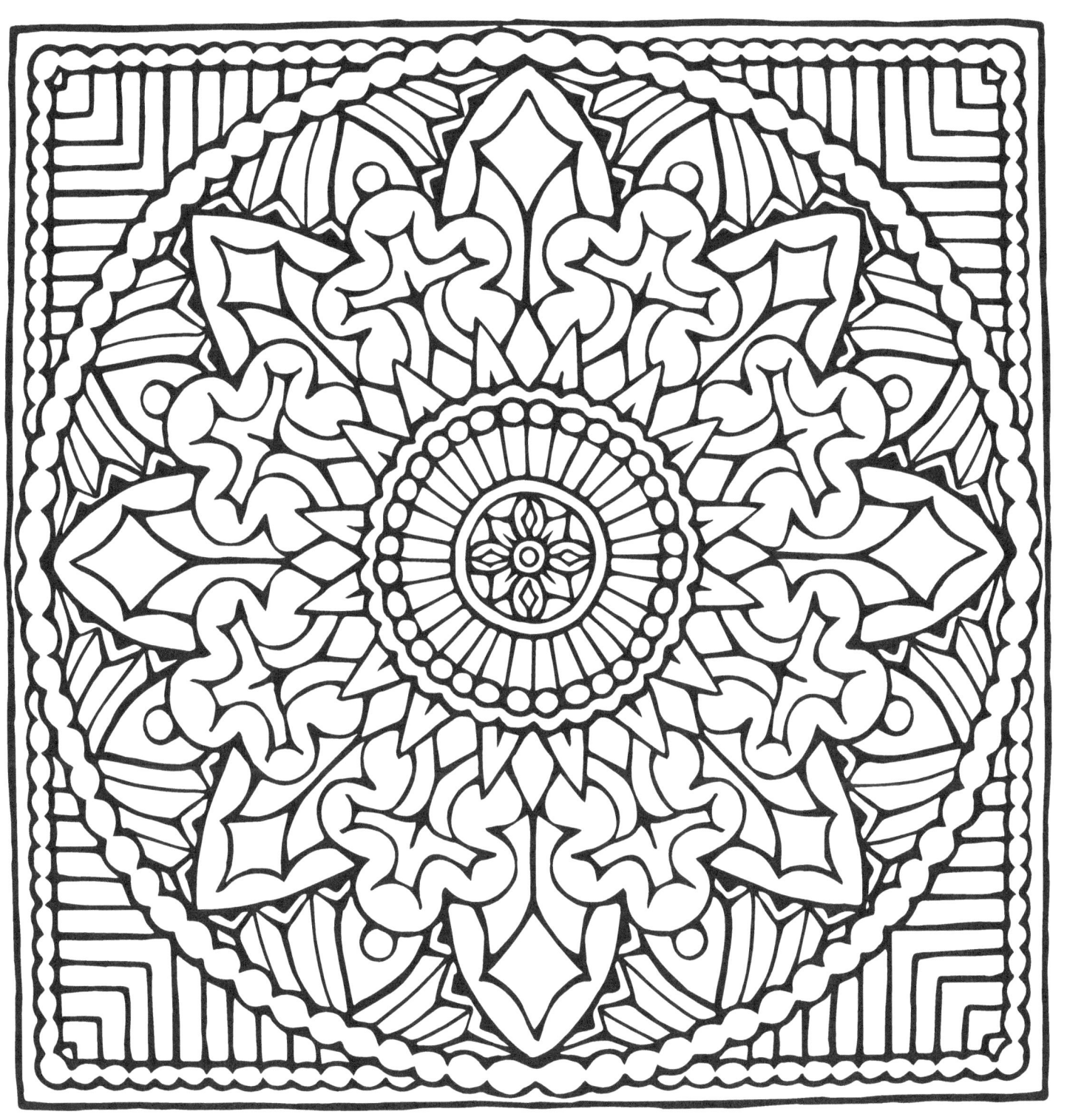

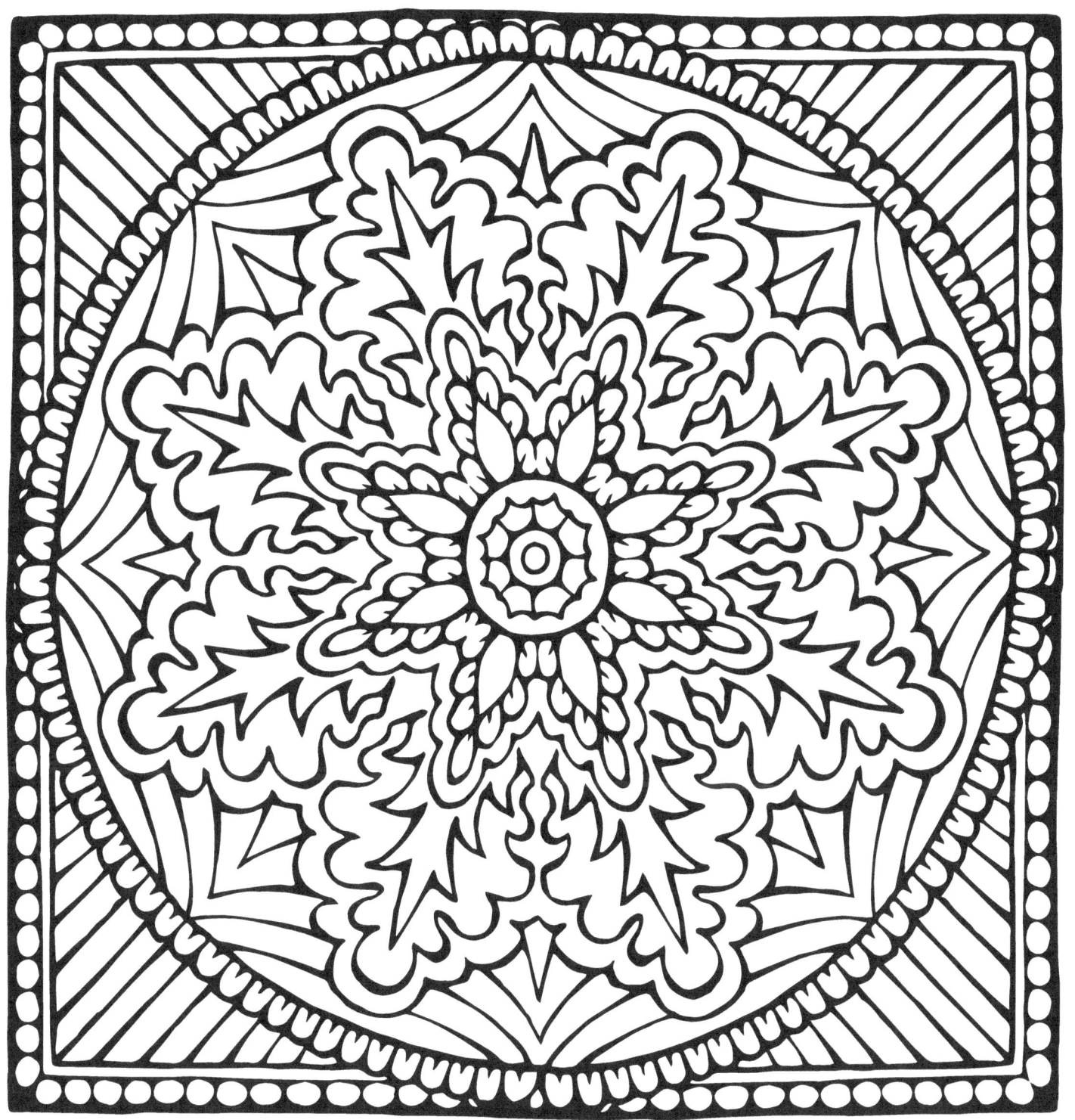

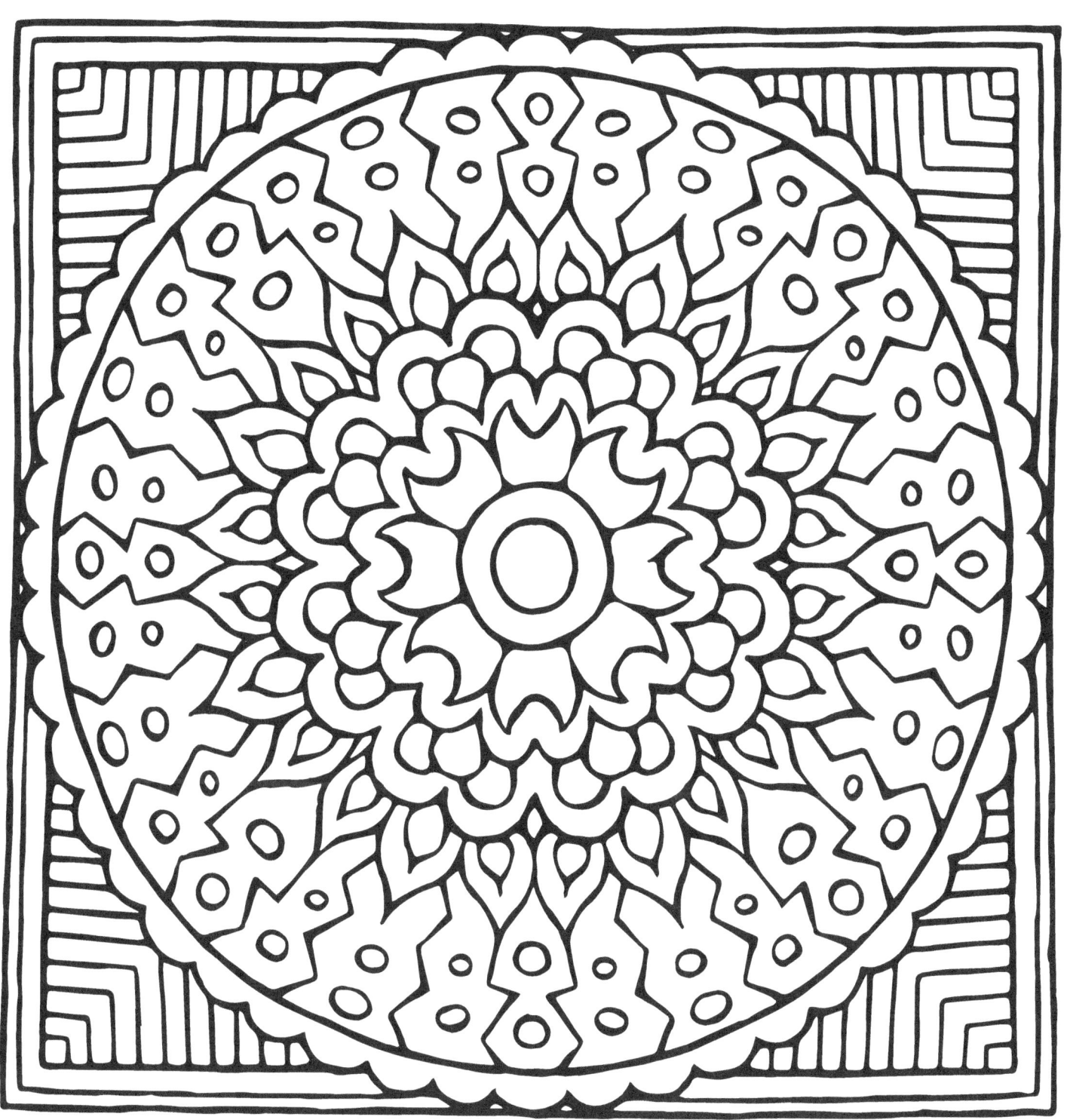

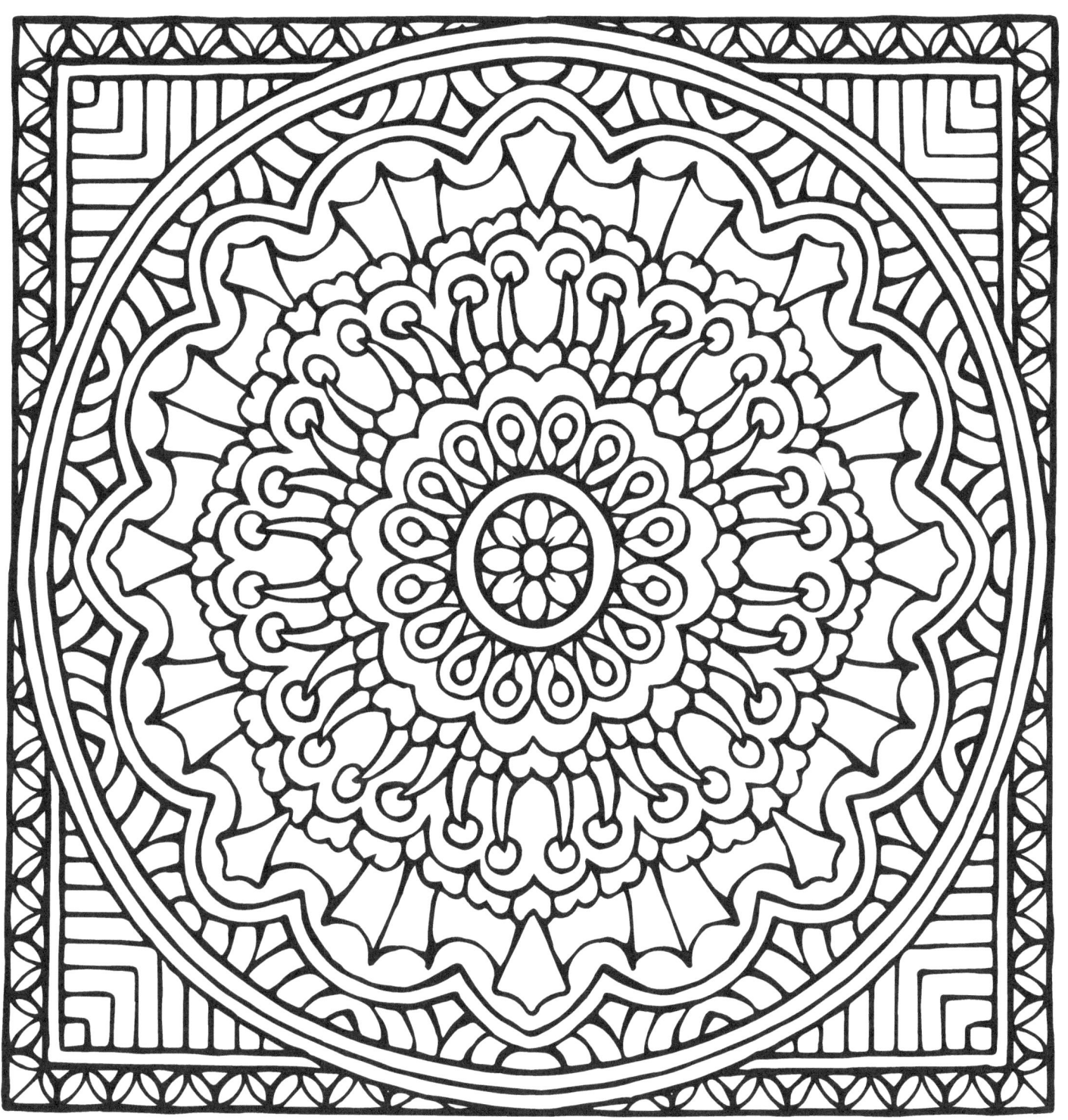

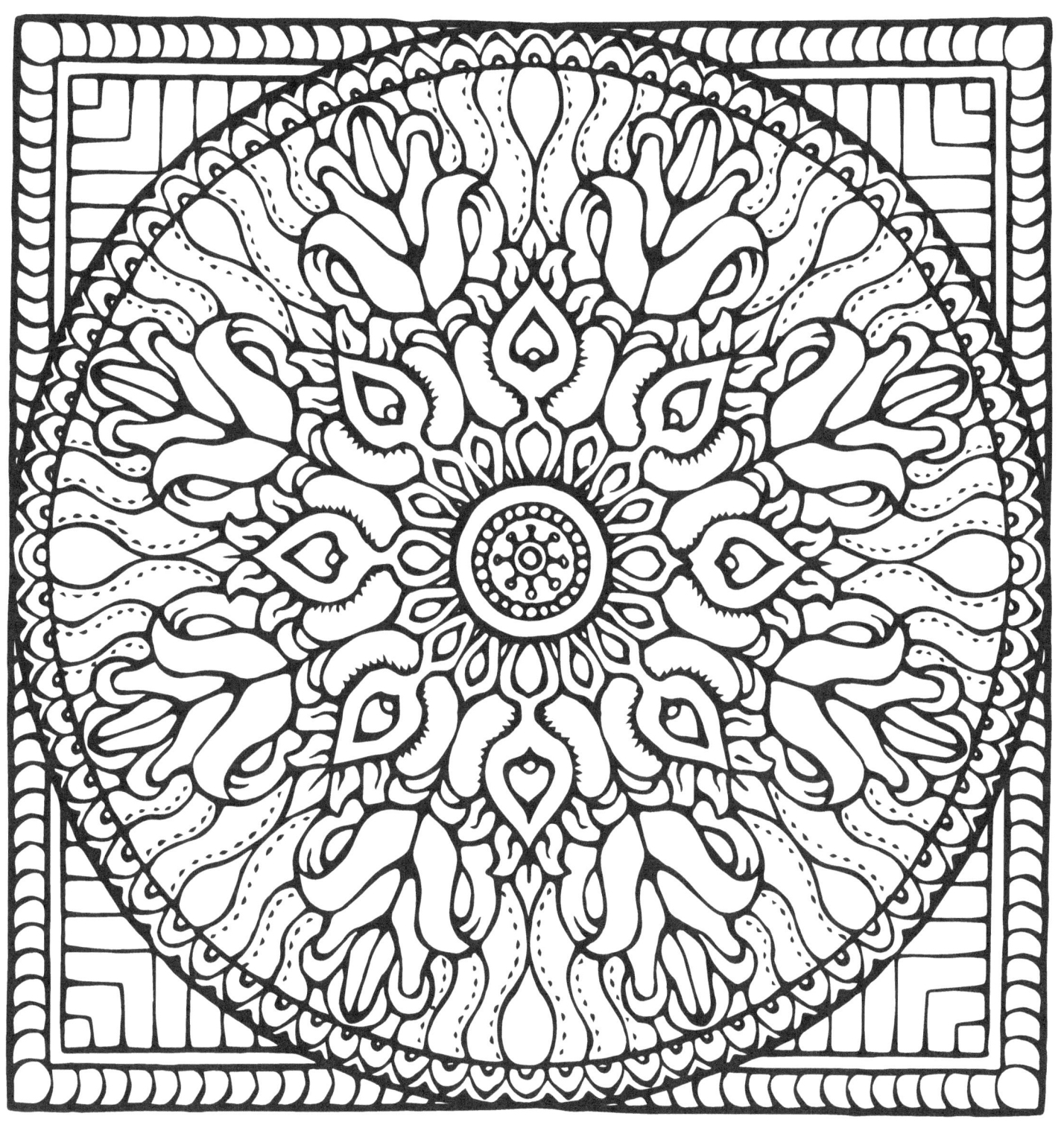

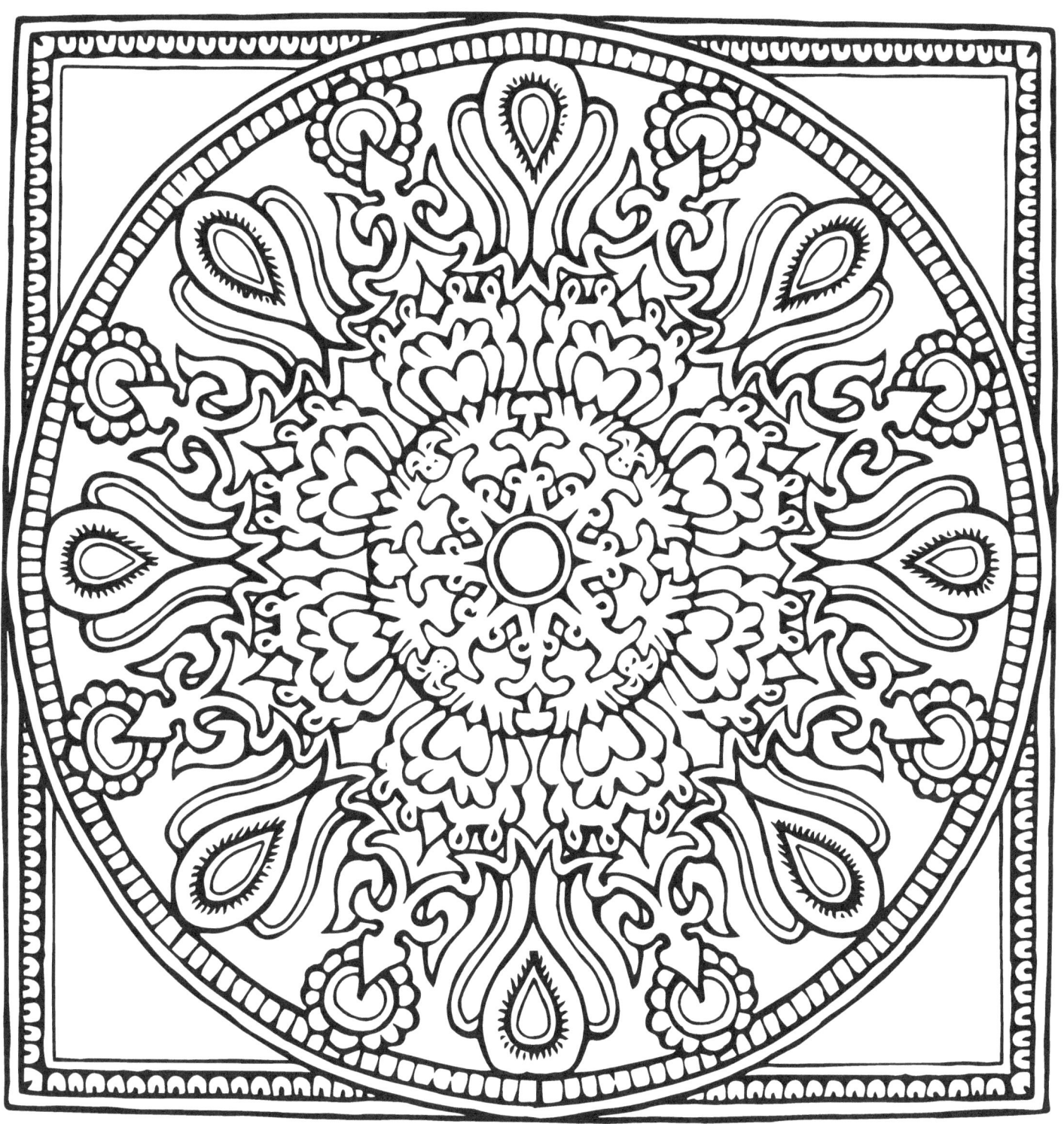

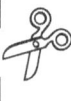 Cut out this page to use as backing, to prevent bleed-through to subsequent pages

Coloring Books by Alberta Hutchinson

Home Made Books Coloring Books

Available from www.createspace.com (see specific web addresses below) and major booksellers:

Mandala Coloring Book Collection:

Mandala Designs Coloring Book No. 1 — 35 New Mandala Designs, (Revised in New Format)
www.createspace.com/4506373

Mandala Designs Coloring Book No. 2 — 32 New Mandala Designs, (Revised in New Format)
www.createspace.com/4555976

Mandala Designs Coloring Book No. 3 — 32 New Mandala Designs, (Revised in New Format)
www.createspace.com/4614672

Mandalas Coloring Book No. 4 — 32 New Unframed Round Mandala Designs,
www.createspace.com/5254882

Mandalas Coloring Book No. 5 — 32 New Mandala Designs, www.createspace.com/5298076

Mandalas Coloring Book No. 6 — 32 New Unframed Round Mandala Designs,
www.createspace.com/5365617

Mandalas Coloring Book No. 7 — 32 New Unframed Round Mandala Designs,
www.createspace.com/5385765

More Hutchinson Design Coloring Books:

Fantasy Flowers Coloring Book No. 1 — 24 Designs in Elaborate Oval Frames,
www.createspace.com/4446137

Fantasy Flowers Coloring Book No. 2 — 32 Designs in Elaborate Square Frames,
www.createspace.com/4485357

Fantasy Flowers Coloring Book No. 3 — 32 Designs in Elaborate Oval-Rectangular Frames,
www.createspace.com/5154200

Snowflake Designs Coloring Book — 24 Designs in Elaborate Frames, www.createspace.com/4446148

64 Christmas Ornaments Coloring Book, www.createspace.com/5186172

Make Your Own Book No. 1 — 50 Elaborate Round Frames for Coloring, with Text Lines,
www.createspace.com/4704942

Make Your Own Book No. 2 — 50 Elaborate Oval Frames for Coloring, www.createspace.com/4765016

Continued on the back...

Coloring Books by Alberta Hutchinson... *Continued*

Dover Publications Coloring Books by Alberta Hutchinson (available from major booksellers):

Mystical Mandala Coloring Book

Infinite Coloring Mandala Design CD and Book, by Martha Bartfeld and Alberta Hutchinson

Creative Haven Square Mandalas (Creative Haven Coloring Books)

Creative Haven Lotus Designs (Creative Haven Coloring Books), by Alberta Hutchinson

3-D Coloring Book - Mandalas, by Martha Bartfeld and Alberta Hutchinson

More Books by Alberta Hutchinson From the Home Made Books Collection

Available from www.createspace.com (see specific web addresses below) and major booksellers:

ILLUSTRATED POETRY:

Fireflies, by Rabindranath Tagore, illustrated by Alberta Hutchinson (color version),
www.createspace.com/5074812 (all proceeds donated to the Ninash Foundation)

Fireflies, by Rabindranath Tagore, illustrated by Alberta Hutchinson (black and white version),
www.createspace.com/5070674 (all proceeds donated to the Ninash Foundation)

Songs of Symmetry, poems and art by Alberta Hutchinson, in full color, www.createspace.com/4019375

CHILDREN'S PICTURE BOOK:

The Orphan and the Christmas Tree, by Edward C. Colwell, illustrated by Alberta Hutchinson,
www.createspace.com/3702633

NOVEL:

Step by Step, by Alberta Hutchinson, www.createspace.com/3669073

BUDDHIST:

100 Meditations on the Sacred Healing Buddha, framed illustrations in full color by Alberta Hutchinson,
www.createspace.com/4938232, (all proceeds donated to Free Tibet)

www.ingramcontent.com/pod-product-compliance
Lightning Source LLC
Chambersburg PA
CBHW081850170526
45167CB00007B/2960